Our Skin

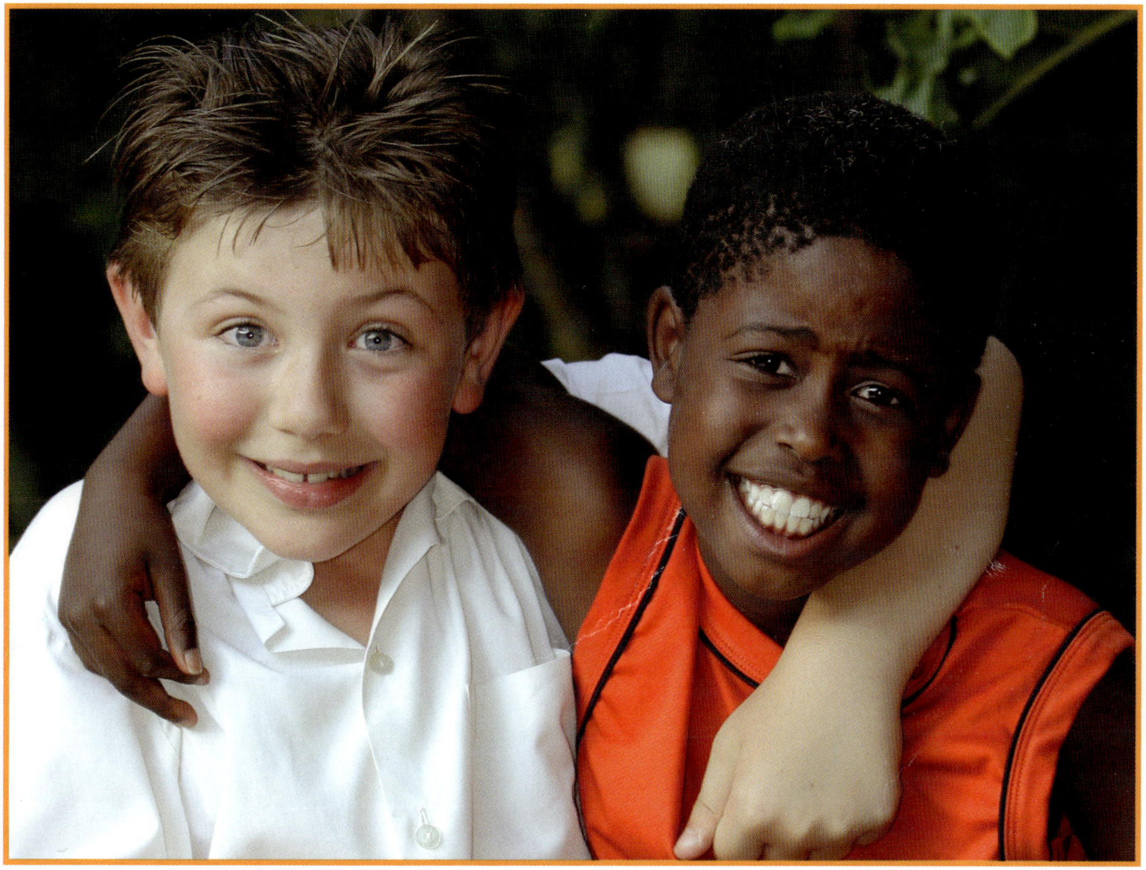

Susan Thames

Publishing LLC
Vero Beach, Florida 32964

© 2008 Rourke Publishing LLC

All rights reserved. No part of this book may be reproduced or utilized in any form or by any means, electronic or mechanical including photocopying, recording, or by any information storage and retrieval system without permission in writing from the publisher.

www.rourkepublishing.com

PHOTO CREDITS: © Cliff Parnell: title page; © Renee Brady: pages 5, 11, 15, 21; © Peeter Viisimaa: page 7; © Sue McDonald: page 13; © Pamela Moore: page 17; © Rob Friedman: page 19.

Editor: Robert Stengard-Olliges

Cover design by Michelle Moore.

Library of Congress Cataloging-in-Publication Data

Thames, Susan.
 Our skin / Susan Thames.
    p. cm. -- (Our bodies)
 Includes bibliographical references and index.
  ISBN 978-1-60044-515-6 (Hardcover)
  ISBN 978-1-60044-676-4 (Softcover)
 1. Skin--Juvenile literature. I. Title.
  QP88.5.T43 2008
  612.7'9--dc22
                               2007011850

Printed in the USA

CG/CG

www.rourkepublishing.com – rourke@rourkepublishing.com
Post Office Box 3328, Vero Beach, FL 32964

Table of Contents

Your Skin   4
What Skin Does   12
Healthy Skin   20
Glossary   23
Index   24

Your Skin

Touch your face.
How does your skin feel?

Your skin is on the outside.

7

The skin on your hands is tight.

The skin on your knees is loose.

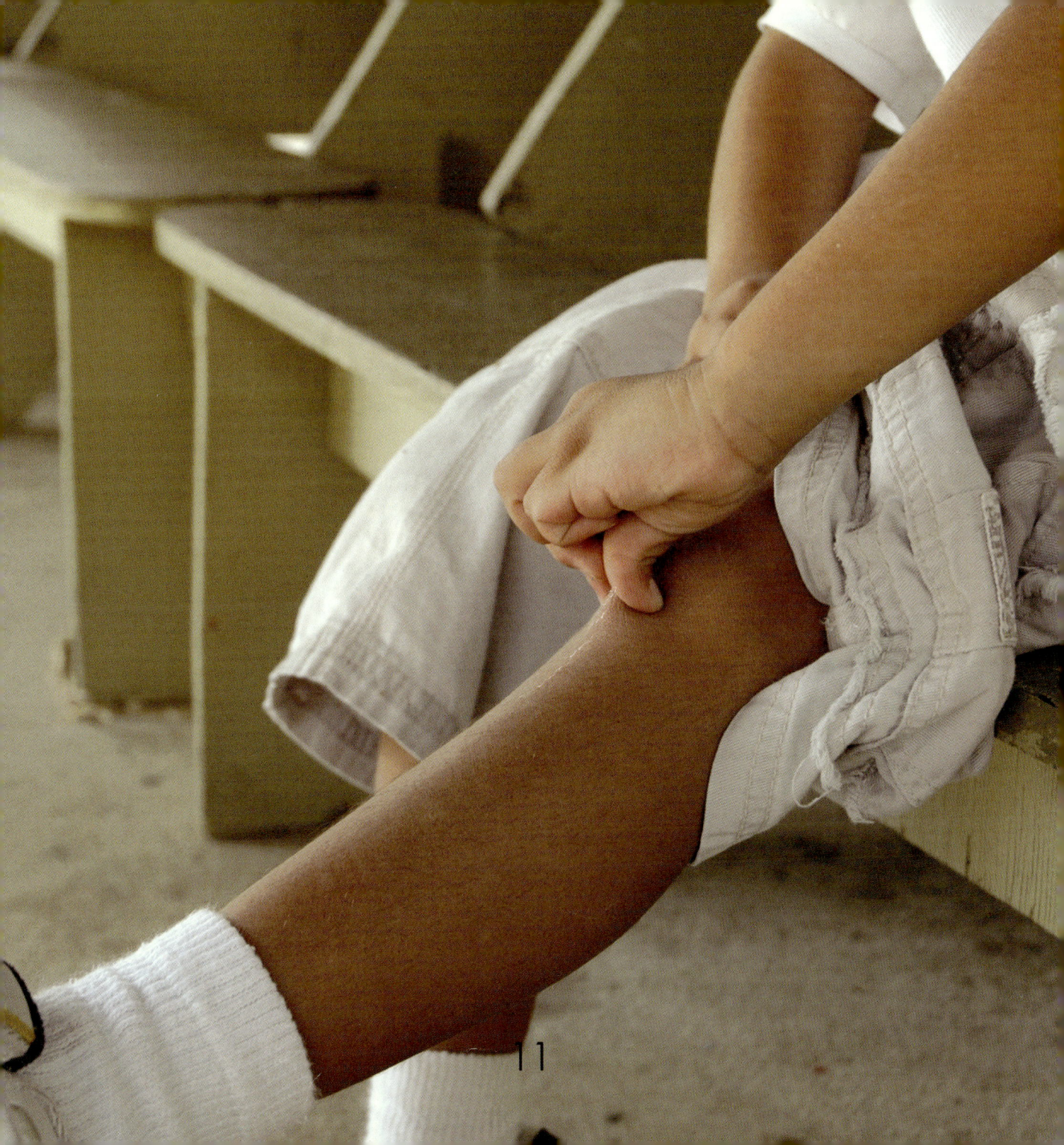

11

What Skin Does

Skin keeps your insides in.

Skin keeps **germs** and dirt out.

Skin is your sense of touch.

Skin **sweats** when you get too hot.

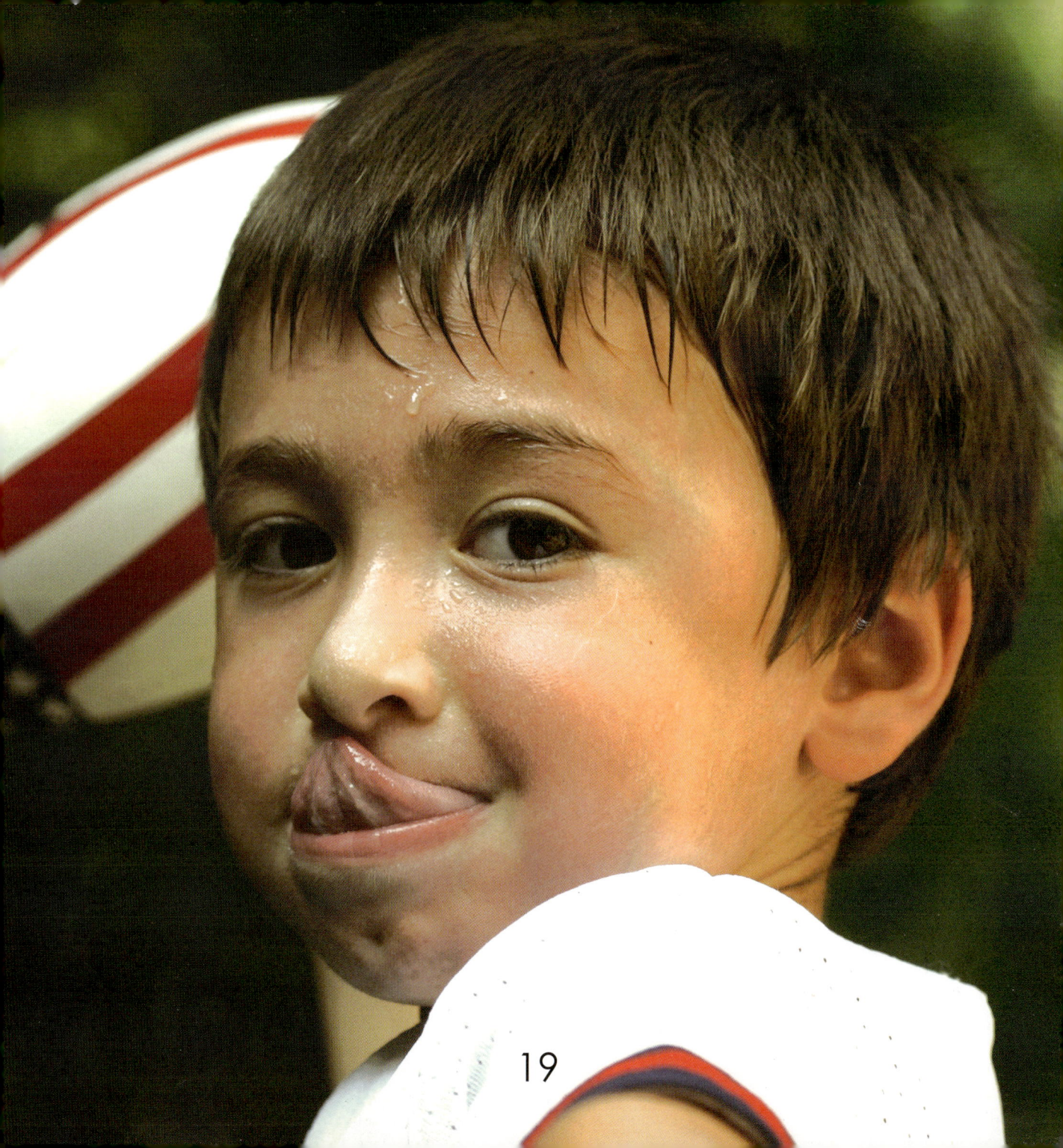

Healthy Skin

Keep your skin clean.

Use **sunscreen** on your skin.

Glossary

germs (JURMZ) — tiny living things that can make you sick

sunscreen (SUHN skreen) — lotion to prevent sunburn

sweat (SWET) — water that comes from your skin when you get hot

Index

clean 20
dirt 14
touch 4, 16

Further Reading

Degezelle, Terri. *Taking Care of My Skin*. Pebble Plus, 2006.

Gray, Susan H. *The Skin*. The Child's World, 2006.

Websites to Visit

www.kidshealth.org
www.healthfinder.gov/kids
www.yucky.discovery.com

About the Author

Susan Thames, a former elementary school teacher, lives in Tampa, Florida. She enjoys spending time with her grandsons and hopes to instill in them a love of reading and a passion for travel.